Table of Contents

ASTRO BOY

19

by
Osamu Tezuka

translation
Frederik L. Schodt

lettering and retouch
Sno Cone Studios

Dark Horse Manga™

publisher
MIKE RICHARDSON

editor
CHRIS WARNER

consulting editor
TOREN SMITH for STUDIO PROTEUS

collection designers
DAVID NESTELLE and LANI SCHREIBSTEIN

English-language version produced by **DARK HORSE COMICS** and **STUDIO PROTEUS**

ASTRO BOY® VOLUME 19

The artwork of this volume has been produced as a mirror-image of the original Japanese edition to conform to English-language standards.

Published by
Dark Horse Manga
A division of Dark Horse Comics, Inc.
10956 SE Main Street
Milwaukie, OR 97222

WWW.DARKHORSE.COM

To find a comics shop in your area, call the Comic Shop Locator Service toll-free at 1-888-266-4226.

First edition: September 2003
ISBN: 1-56971-900-4

10 9 8 7 6 5 4 3 2 1
Printed in Canada

A NOTE TO READERS

Many non-Japanese, including people from Africa and Southeast Asia, appear in Osamu Tezuka's works. Sometimes these people are depicted very differently from the way they actually are today, in a manner that exaggerates a time long past or shows them to be from extremely undeveloped lands. Some feel that such images contribute to racial discrimination, especially against people of African descent. This was never Osamu Tezuka's intent, but we believe that as long as there are people who feel insulted or demeaned by these depictions, we must not ignore their feelings.

We are against discrimination, in all its forms, and intend to continue to work for its elimination. Nonetheless, we do not believe it would be proper to revise these works. Tezuka is no longer with us, and we cannot erase what he has done, and to alter his work would only violate his rights as a creator. More importantly, stopping publication or changing the content of his work would do little to solve the problems of discrimination that exist in the world.

We are presenting Osamu Tezuka's work as it was originally created, without changes. We do this because we believe it is also important to promote the underlying themes in his work, such as love for mankind and the sanctity of life. We hope that when you, the reader, encounter this work, you will keep in mind the differences in attitudes, then and now, toward discrimination, and that this will contribute to an even greater awareness of such problems.

— Tezuka Productions and Dark Horse Comics

BLUE KNIGHT

First serialized from October 1965 to March 1966 in *Shonen* magazine.

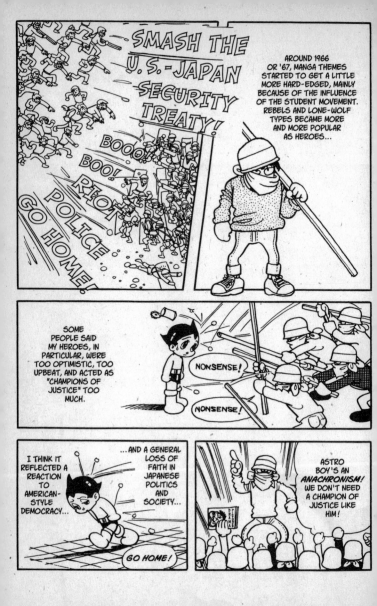

SMASH THE U.S.-JAPAN SECURITY TREATY!

BOO! BOO! RIOT POLICE GO HOME!

AROUND 1966 OR '67, MANGA THEMES STARTED TO GET A LITTLE MORE HARD-EDGED, MAINLY BECAUSE OF THE INFLUENCE OF THE STUDENT MOVEMENT. REBELS AND LONE-WOLF TYPES BECAME MORE AND MORE POPULAR AS HEROES...

SOME PEOPLE SAID MY HEROES, IN PARTICULAR, WERE TOO OPTIMISTIC, TOO UPBEAT, AND ACTED AS "CHAMPIONS OF JUSTICE" TOO MUCH.

NONSENSE!

NONSENSE!

I THINK IT REFLECTED A REACTION TO AMERICAN-STYLE DEMOCRACY...

...AND A GENERAL LOSS OF FAITH IN JAPANESE POLITICS AND SOCIETY...

GO HOME!

ASTRO BOY'S AN ANACHRONISM! WE DON'T NEED A CHAMPION OF JUSTICE LIKE HIM!

8

10

AFTER I CHANGED ASTRO'S PERSONALITY, HIS POPULARITY PLUMMETED BEFORE MY EYES. IT WAS TOO LATE...

HEY, DON'T LOOK AT ME, MAN... IT'S NOT MY FAULT... SEE YA LATER...

Y-YOU *COWARD!!*

ASTRO BOY WILL *ALWAYS* BE A CHAMPION OF JUSTICE!

GOSH, DR. TEZUKA... I WANNA BE LIKE I USED TO BE... I WANNA BE A FRIEND TO HUMANS...

DON'T WORRY, ASTRO... I'LL NEVER BE SWAYED LIKE THAT AGAIN!

THE STUDENT MOVEMENT EVENTUALLY DIED DOWN, BUT EVEN ASTRO HAD BEEN SWEPT UP IN THE EMOTIONS OF THE TIMES...

SO I MADE ASTRO AGAIN LIKE HE USED TO BE -- A *CHAMPION OF JUSTICE*... BUT IT WAS HARD FOR HIM TO GET HIS POPULARITY BACK...

11

12

13

14

15

18

19

"ROBOTS AREN'T ALLOWED TO GO OVERSEAS WITHOUT PERMISSION!"

I WANNA BE RE-BORN AS A ♀!

"AND MALE AND FEMALE ROBOTS AREN'T ALLOWED TO SWITCH GENDER!"

"ROBOTS AREN'T ALLOWED TO CHANGE FACES WITHOUT PERMISSION OR TO ADOPT OTHER IDENTITIES..."

"ROBOTS ORIGINALLY MADE AS ADULTS AREN'T ALLOWED TO BECOME CHILDREN!"

"ROBOTS AREN'T ALLOWED TO PUT BACK TOGETHER ROBOTS THAT HUMANS HAVE TAKEN APART!"

"ROBOTS AREN'T ALLOWED TO SMASH HUMAN HOUSES OR TOOLS!"

THE ROBOT LAW FORBIDS ALL THESE THINGS!

BUT I'VE HAD ENOUGH!

I'VE DECIDED TO SMASH THE ROBOT LAW FOR ONCE AND FOR ALL, DR. LOS!

B-BUT THAT'S CRAZY! YOU'VE GOT TO STOP!

EVEN HUMANS HAVE TO OBEY LAWS! AND THEY DO!!

21

22

23

24

25

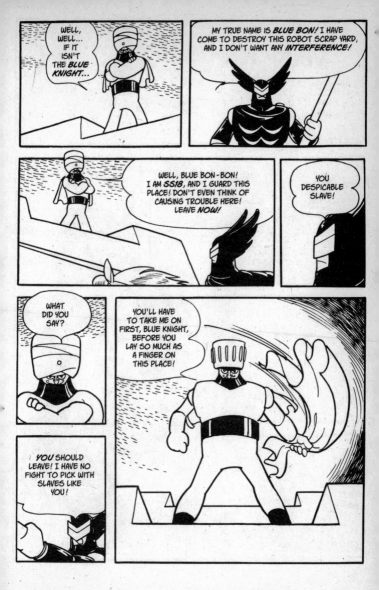

30

CLIPPITY CLOP CLIPPITY CLOP

THE MOST ADVANCED ROBOT RE-PROCESSING CENTER IN ASIA, IN THE SUBURBS OF NEW DELHI, IN INDIA, HAS BEEN ATTACKED!

THE CULPRIT IS BELIEVED TO BE NONE OTHER THAN BLUE KNIGHT, WHO HAS BEEN IN THE NEWS SO MUCH LATELY. AFTER SMASHING THE PLANT, HE VANISHED WITHOUT A TRACE!

THE BLUE KNIGHT HAS THUS FAR ATTACKED OVER THIRTY-THREE PLACES AROUND THE WORLD!

WHERE WILL HE APPEAR NEXT?! THIS VERY MOMENT, POLICE DEPARTMENTS AROUND THE WORLD ARE DESPERATELY SEARCHING FOR HIM!

WHO'S THE BLUE KNIGHT, ASTRO?

NOBODY REALLY KNOWS YET, URAN...

IS HE A GOOD ROBOT OR A BAD ONE? A FRIEND OR AN ENEMY?

DON'T ASK SO MANY QUESTIONS, URAN! IT'S TIME TO GO TO SLEEP!

31

34

36

39

40

41

42

43

44

45

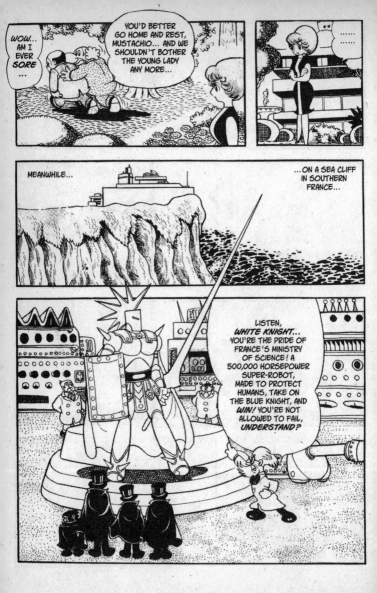

47

48

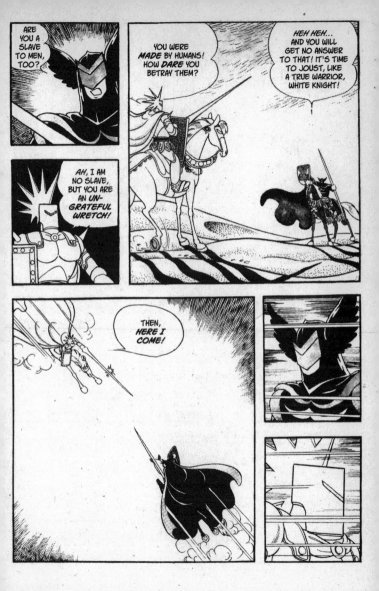

49

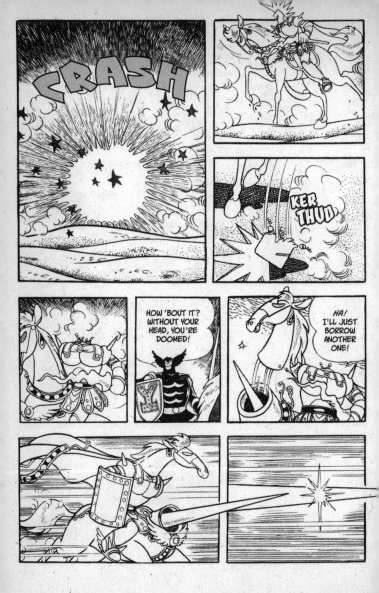

51

52

53

54

IF IT'S A PROBLEM, TRY THIS ONE!
WELL? HOW 'BOUT IT?! DOES IT DO THE SAME THING?
NO, THIS TIME IT'S FINE...
IT'S JUST AN ORDINARY OLD SWORD... EN GARDE, ASTRO!
REMEMBER NOW, IF I WIN, YOU HAVE TO JOIN ME! IF I LOSE, YOU CAN DO WITH ME AS YOU PLEASE!
BUT I'M NOT GOING TO LOSE...
HERE I COME!!

59

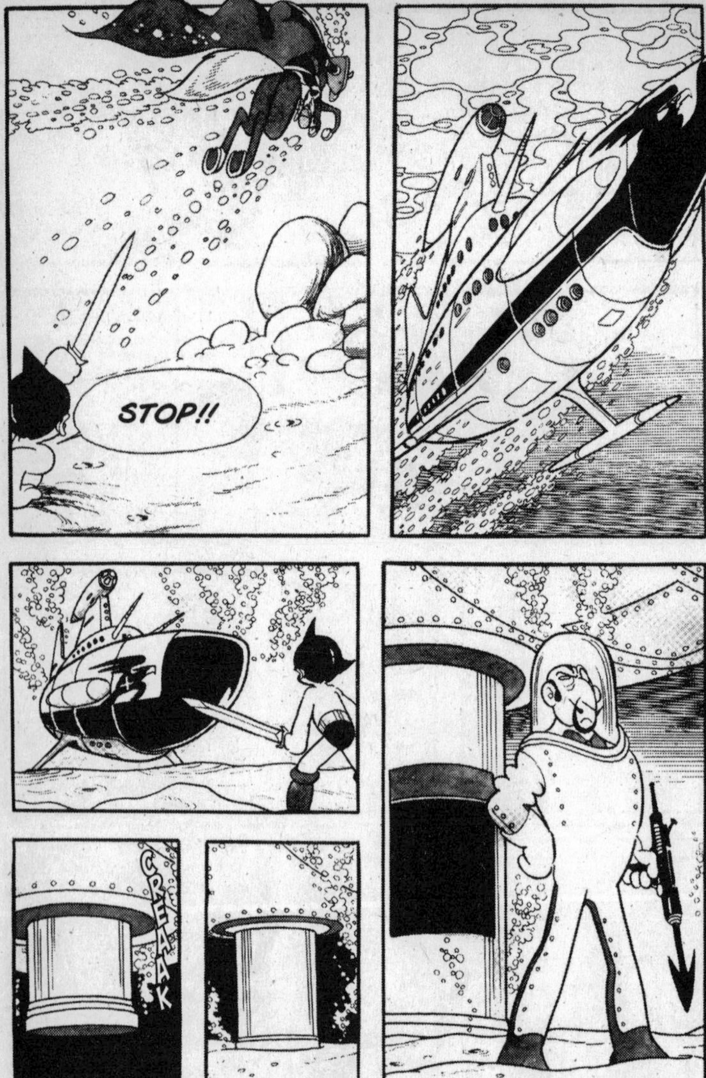
STOP!!
CREAAK

TONTO!!

WHA?!

TONTO! YOU'RE THE BLUE KNIGHT, AREN'T YOU!? WHAT'S GOING ON?

WHAT'RE YOU TALKING ABOUT?! I DIDN'T DO ANYTHING!

WHO DO YOU THINK YOU'RE KIDDING!!? WE WERE *DUELING* UNDER THE OCEAN YESTERDAY!!

UNDER THE *OCEAN*? B-BUT I DIDN'T GO *ANYWHERE*!

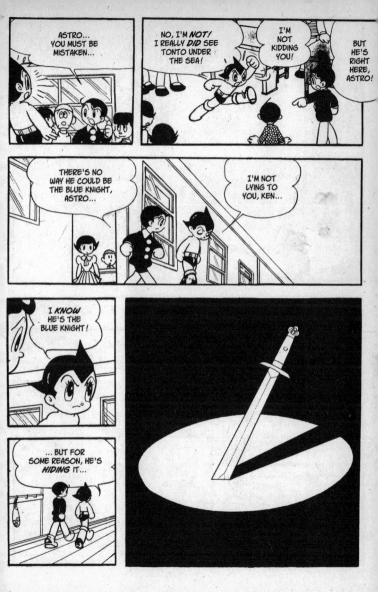

ASTRO... YOU MUST BE MISTAKEN...

NO, I'M *NOT!* I REALLY *DID* SEE TONTO UNDER THE SEA!

I'M NOT KIDDING YOU!

BUT HE'S RIGHT HERE, ASTRO!

THERE'S NO WAY HE COULD BE THE BLUE KNIGHT, ASTRO...

I'M NOT LYING TO YOU, KEN...

I *KNOW* HE'S THE BLUE KNIGHT!

... BUT FOR SOME REASON, HE'S *HIDING* IT...

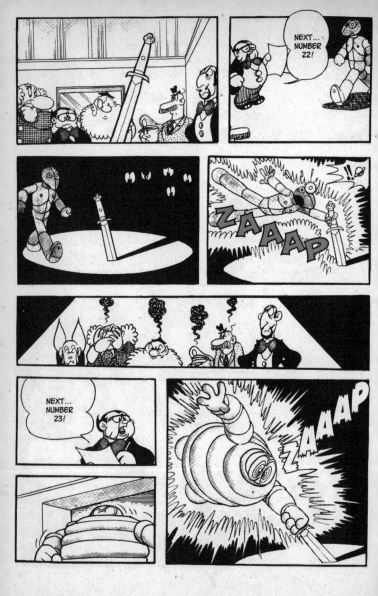

67

SOME ROBOTS *CAN* HOLD THIS SWORD, AND SOME *CAN'T*...

GENTLEMEN, THIS IS AN EXTREMELY IMPORTANT FACT!

IT MEANS THE SWORD IS DESIGNED SO ONLY CERTAIN MODELS OF ROBOTS CAN USE IT!

B...BUT WHAT KIND OF MODELS?

THOSE LIKE THE *BLUE KNIGHT!*

DANGEROUS ROBOTS! THE KIND THAT DON'T RESPECT HUMANS AND STRIKE THEM WITH NO COMPUNCTION!

B..BUT...

WE'RE GOT A REAL PROBLEM, PROFESSOR OCHANOMIZU! BASICALLY, YOU ROBOTOLOGISTS HAVE UNWITTINGLY MADE A GRAVE ERROR!

B-BUT WE DON'T MAKE ROBOTS LIKE THAT AT THE MINISTRY OF SCIENCE!

THAT'S WHY I SAID, "UNWITTINGLY"!

I'M CERTAIN THERE ARE MANY ROBOTS LIKE THE BLUE KNIGHT IN THE WORLD!

WITH TONS OF 'EM RUNNING AROUND, WE COULD HAVE A *DISASTER!*

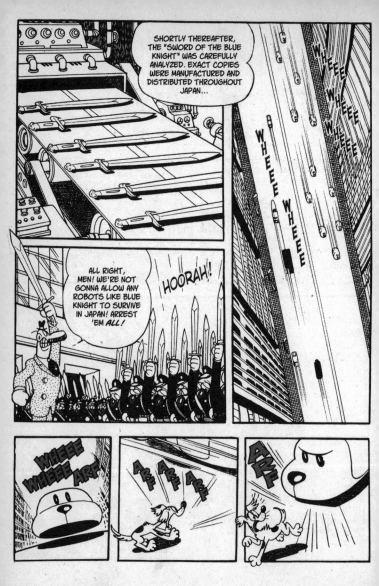

72

74

75

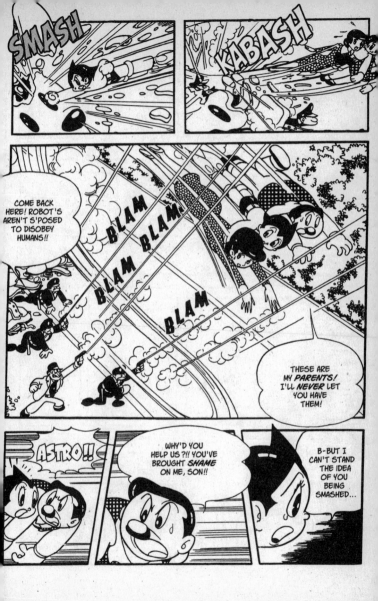

78

79

81

83

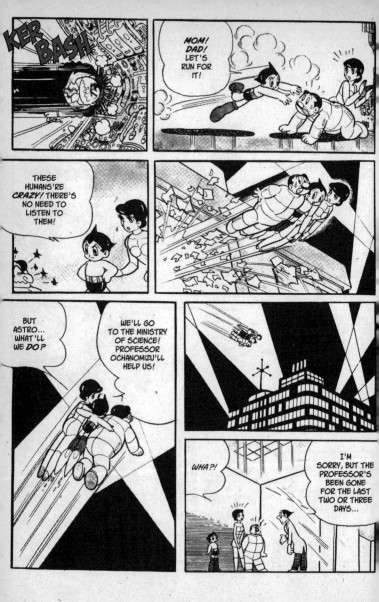

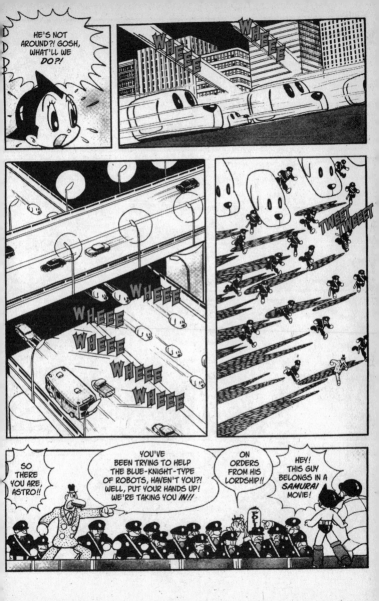

86

88

89

91

93

94

98

CLANKETY CLANKETY CLANKETY CLANKETY CLANKETY CLANKETY CLANKETY CLANKETY

TRA LA TRA LA TRA LA TRA LA...

HI, MR. CUZCO! HERE'S SOME FLOWERS FOR YOU!

WE'LL SOON HAVE *BUILDINGS* HERE INSTEAD OF FIELDS OF FLOWERS, URAN...

IT'LL BE THE CAPITAL OF ROBOT-ANIA!

BUT I LIKE THIS FIELD THE WAY IT IS!

BUT WE ROBOTS DON'T NEED THIS FOR OUR CAPITAL!

WHAT'S THE MATTER WITH YOU, MISTER... DON'T YOU LIKE FLOWERS ?!

I DON'T DISLIKE THEM... BUT WE CAN MAKE *ROBOT* FLOWERS!!

102

103

107

109

110

115

117

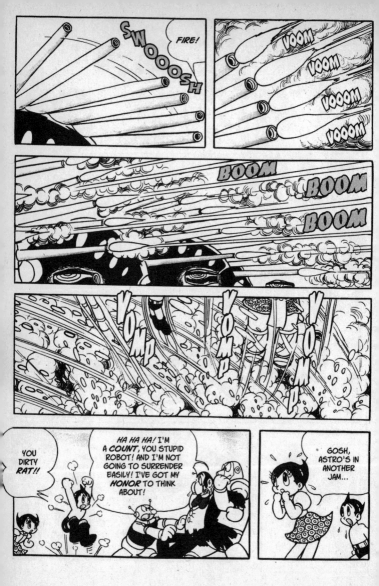

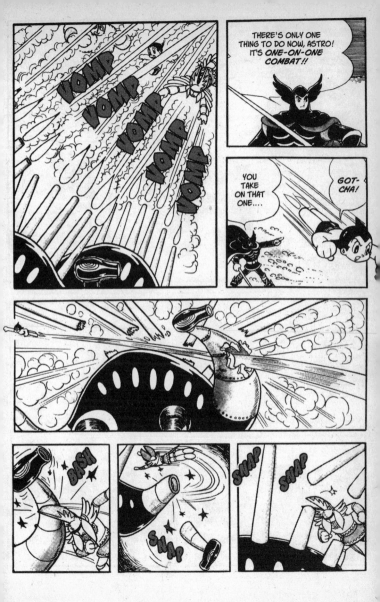

123

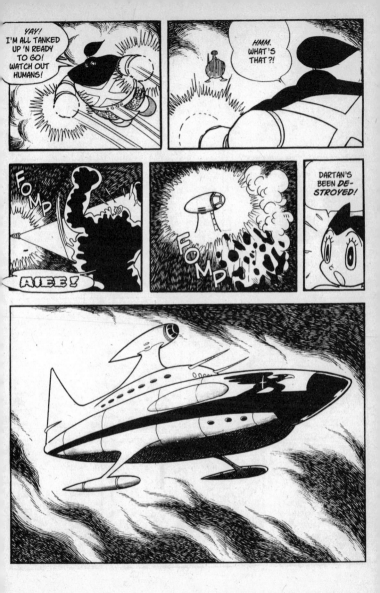

125

127

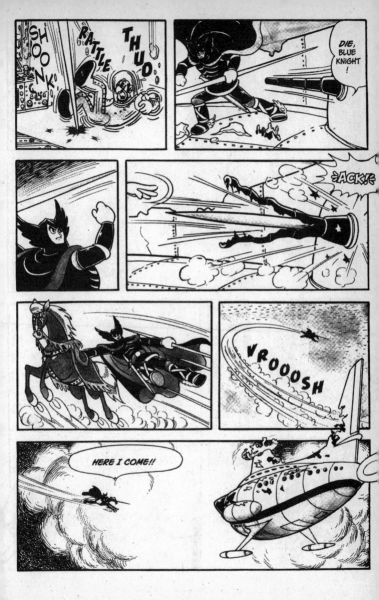

132

133

TONTO...
FORGIVE ME,
PLEASE...

135

137

138

140

141

142

143

145

146

147

149

151

152

153

155

157

158

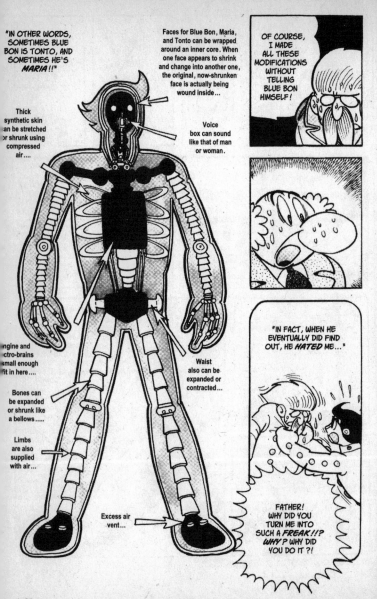

"IN OTHER WORDS, SOMETIMES BLUE BON IS TONTO, AND SOMETIMES HE'S *MARIA*!!"

Thick synthetic skin can be stretched or shrunk using compressed air....

Faces for Blue Bon, Maria, and Tonto can be wrapped around an inner core. When one face appears to shrink and change into another one, the original, now-shrunken face is actually being wound inside...

Voice box can sound like that of man or woman.

ngine and ctro-brains small enough fit in here....

Bones can be expanded or shrunk like a bellows.....

Limbs are also supplied with air...

Waist also can be expanded or contracted...

Excess air vent...

OF COURSE, I MADE ALL THESE MODIFICATIONS WITHOUT TELLING BLUE BON HIMSELF!

"IN FACT, WHEN HE EVENTUALLY DID FIND OUT, HE *HATED* ME..."

FATHER! WHY DID YOU TURN ME INTO SUCH A *FREAK*!!? *WHY*? WHY DID YOU DO IT?!

161

163

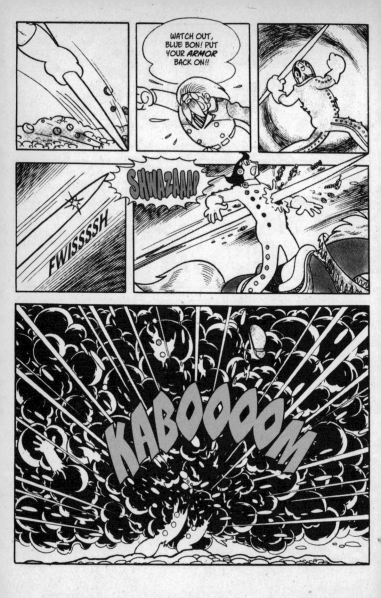

ASTRO BOY REBORN

First serialized from March to May 1966 in *Shonen* magazine.

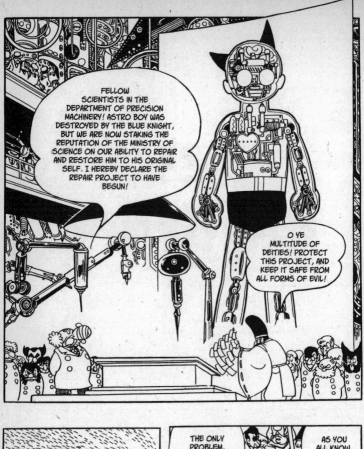

FELLOW SCIENTISTS IN THE DEPARTMENT OF PRECISION MACHINERY! ASTRO BOY WAS DESTROYED BY THE BLUE KNIGHT, BUT WE ARE NOW STAKING THE REPUTATION OF THE MINISTRY OF SCIENCE ON OUR ABILITY TO REPAIR AND RESTORE HIM TO HIS ORIGINAL SELF. I HEREBY DECLARE THE REPAIR PROJECT TO HAVE BEGUN!

O YE MULTITUDE OF DEITIES! PROTECT THIS PROJECT, AND KEEP IT SAFE FROM ALL FORMS OF EVIL!

THE ONLY PROBLEM, GENTLEMEN, IS THAT WE'RE GOING TO NEED *DR. TENMA* TO MAKE THIS REPAIR PROJECT SUCCEED....

AS YOU ALL KNOW, *HE'S* THE ONE WHO ACTUALLY CREATED ASTRO...

172

YOU WANT ASTRO REPAIRED, RIGHT? WELL, GIVE HIM TO ME AND *I'LL* REPAIR HIM. BUT IF I REPAIR HIM, HE'S *MINE TO KEEP!* I'LL MAKE HIM MY REAL *SON!* HOW 'BOUT IT, MR. HEAD OF THE MINISTRY OF SCIENCE?!

B-BUT YOUR DEMANDS ARE *IMPOSSIBLE!!*

A MONTH LATER.... PROFESSOR OCHANOMIZU AND THE REST OF THE MINISTRY OF SCIENCE HAVE POOLED THEIR TALENTS AND EFFORTS, AND FINALLY FINISHED RESTORING ASTRO BOY TO HIS ORIGINAL FORM.

AND NOW, AT LONG LAST, THE DAY HAS COME TO TURN ON ASTRO'S POWER. LADIES AND GENTLEMEN, THE SWITCH HAS BEEN *TURNED ON...*

BZZ BEEP BZZ BEEP BZZ

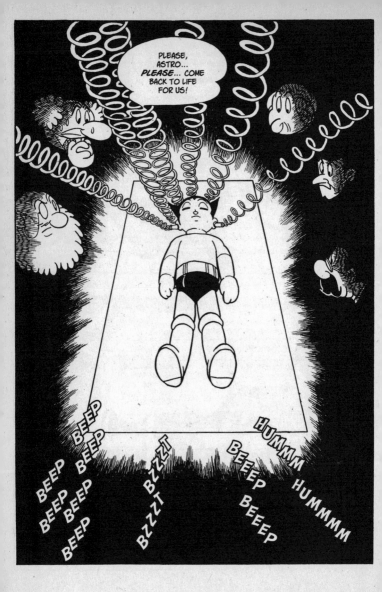

174

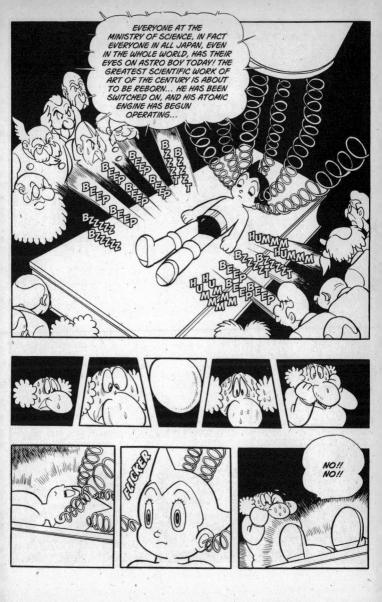

175

177

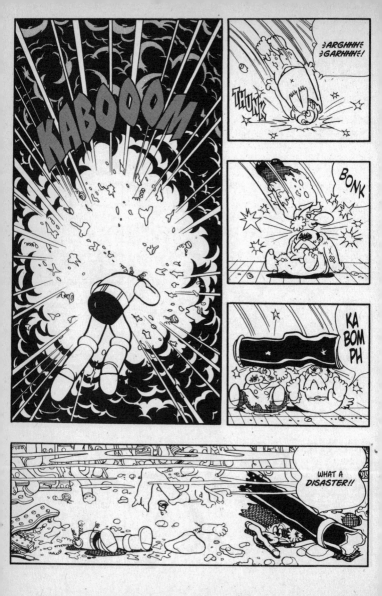

178

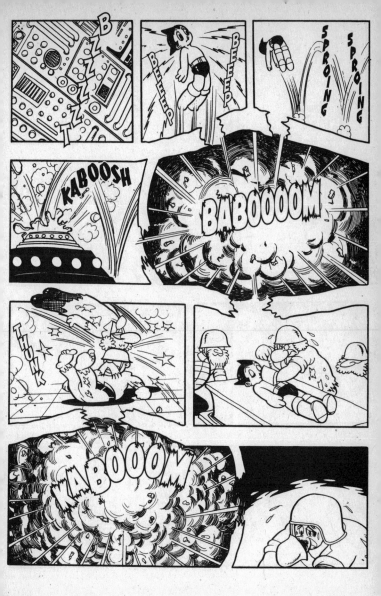

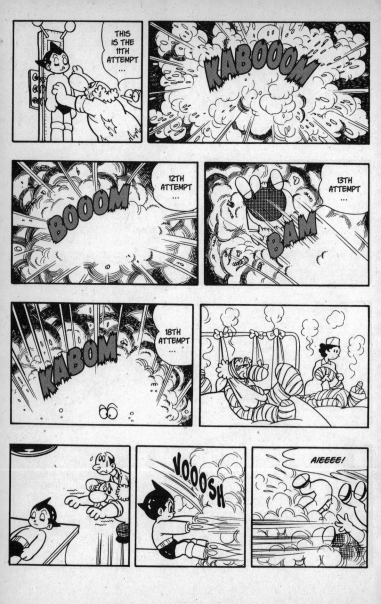

182

VOOOOSH

AIEEE!

WHAT'D HE DO *THIS* TIME?

H-H-HE WAS BREATH-ING *FIRE!!*

BRING IN A GUARD ROBOT! *QUICK!*

YOU'VE GOTTA RESTRAIN ASTRO BOY! WE'RE COUNTING ON YOU!

ASTRO'S GOT ONE MILLION HORSE-POWER... THIS MIGHT NOT WORK...

CALM DOWN, ASTRO BOY!

GUESS THAT DIDN'T WORK....

183

189

190

192

193

195

GAV-
ONK

YOU CAN WATCH FROM IN THERE! HA HA!

≥ARGH≤
≥ARGH≤
≥ARGH≤
≥ARGH≤

HERE WE GO, ASTRO...

CHAK

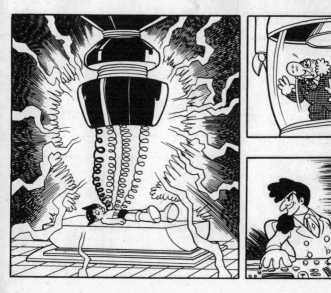

197

202

204

TO BE CONTINUED...

AKIRA
Katsuhiro Otomo
BOOK 1
ISBN: 1-56971-498-3 $24.95
BOOK 2
ISBN: 1-56971-499-1 $24.95
BOOK 3
ISBN: 1-56971-525-4 $24.95
BOOK 4
ISBN: 1-56971-526-2 $27.95
BOOK 5
ISBN: 1-56971-527-0 $27.95
BOOK 6
ISBN: 1-56971-528-9 $29.95

APPLESEED
Masamune Shirow
BOOK ONE
ISBN: 1-56971-070-8 $16.95
BOOK TWO
ISBN: 1-56971-071-6 $16.95
BOOK THREE
ISBN: 1-56971-072-4 $17.95
BOOK FOUR
ISBN: 1-56971-074-0 $17.95

BLACK MAGIC
Masamune Shirow
ISBN: 1-56971-360-X $16.95

BLADE OF THE IMMORTAL
Hiroaki Samura
BLOOD OF A THOUSAND
ISBN: 1-56971-239-5 $14.95
CRY OF THE WORM
ISBN: 1-56971-300-6 $14.95
DREAMSONG
ISBN: 1-56971-357-X $14.95
ON SILENT WINGS
ISBN: 1-56971-412-6 $14.95
ON SILENT WINGS II
ISBN: 1-56971-444-4 $14.95
DARK SHADOWS
ISBN: 1-56971-469-X $14.95
HEART OF DARKNESS
ISBN: 1-56971-531-9 $16.95
THE GATHERING
ISBN: 1-56971-546-7 $15.95
THE GATHERING II
ISBN: 1-56971-560-2 $15.95
BEASTS
ISBN: 1-56971-741-9 $14.95

BUBBLEGUM CRISIS
Adam Warren • Toren Smith
GRAND MAL
ISBN: 1-56971-120-8 $14.95

CANNON GOD EXAXXION
Kenichi Sonoda
VOLUME 1
ISBN: 1-56971-745-1 $15.95

CARAVAN KIDD
Johji Manabe
VOLUME 1
ISBN: 1-56971-260-3 $19.95
VOLUME 2
ISBN: 1-56971-324-3 $19.95
VOLUME 3
ISBN: 1-56971-338-3 $19.95

THE DIRTY PAIR
Adam Warren • Toren Smith
BIOHAZARDS
ISBN: 1-56971-339-1 $12.95
DANGEROUS ACQUAINTANCES
ISBN: 1-56971-227-1 $12.95
A PLAGUE OF ANGELS
ISBN: 1-56971-029-5 $12.95
SIM HELL
ISBN: 1-56971-742-7 $13.95
FATAL BUT NOT SERIOUS
ISBN: 1-56971-172-0 $14.95

DOMINION
Masamune Shirow
ISBN: 1-56971-488-6 $16.95

DOMU: A CHILD'S DREAM
Katsuhiro Otomo
ISBN: 1-56971-611-0 $17.95

GHOST IN THE SHELL
Masamune Shirow
ISBN: 1-56971-081-3 $24.95

GUNSMITH CATS
Kenichi Sonoda
BONNIE AND CLYDE
ISBN: 1-56971-215-8 $13.95

MISFIRE
ISBN: 1-56971-253-0 $14.95
THE RETURN OF GRAY
ISBN: 1-56971-299-9 $17.95
GOLDIE VS. MISTY
ISBN: 1-56971-371-5 $15.95
BAD TRIP
ISBN: 1-56971-442-8 $13.95
BEAN BANDIT
ISBN: 1-56971-453-3 $16.95
KIDNAPPED
ISBN: 1-56971-529-7 $16.95
MR. V
ISBN: 1-56971-550-5 $18.95
MISTY'S RUN
ISBN: 1-56971-684-6 $14.95

INTRON DEPOT
Masamune Shirow
INTRON DEPOT 1
ISBN: 1-56971-085-6 $39.95
INTRON DEPOT 2: BLADES
ISBN: 1-56971-382-0 $39.95

LONE WOLF AND CUB
Kazuo Koike & Goseki Kojima
VOLUME 1: THE ASSASSIN'S ROAD
ISBN: 1-56971-502-5 $9.95
VOLUME 2: THE GATELESS BARRIER
ISBN: 1-56971-503-3 $9.95
VOLUME 3: THE FLUTE OF THE FALLEN TIGER
ISBN: 1-56971-504-1 $9.95
VOLUME 4: THE BELL WARDEN
ISBN: 1-56971-505-X $9.95
VOLUME 5: BLACK WIND
ISBN: 1-5671-506-8 $9.95
VOLUME 6: LANTERNS FOR THE DEAD
ISBN: 1-56971-507-6 $9.95
VOLUME 7: CLOUD DRAGON, WIND TIGER
ISBN: 1-56971-508-4 $9.95
VOLUME 8: CHAINS OF DEATH
ISBN: 1-56971-509-2 $9.95
VOLUME 9: ECHO OF THE ASSASSIN
ISBN: 1-56971-510-6 $9.95
VOLUME 10: HOSTAGE CHILD
ISBN: 1-56971-511-4 $9.95